WRITER'S NOTEBOOK

THE WHOLE TRUTH

Writing Fearless Nonfiction

NPL|F
Nashville Public Library | FOUNDATION

*This book given
to the Nashville Public Library
through the generosity of the*
**Dollar General
Literacy Foundation**

NPLF.ORG

CAPSTONE PRESS

Savvy Books are published by Capstone Press,
1710 Roe Crest Drive, North Mankato, Minnesota 56003
www.capstonepub.com

Library of Congress Cataloging-in-Publication Data
Higgins, Nadia.
The whole truth : writing fearless nonfiction / by Nadia Higgins.
    P. cm. Includes bibliographical references and index.
Summary: "Introduces and defines essential elements of writing
nonfiction accompanied by compelling writing prompts for practicing new
skills. Real-life author bios and excerpts enhance skills and
understanding"-- Provided by publisher.
 ISBN 978-1-4914-5989-8 (hardcover : alk. paper) --
ISBN 978-1-4914-5993-5 (pbk. : alk. paper) -- ISBN 978-1-4914-5997-3 (ebook
pdf) 1. Creative nonfiction--Authorship--Juvenile literature. I. Title.
PN145.H524 2016
808.02--dc23 2015013882

Editorial Credits
Jeni Wittrock, editor; Veronica Scott, designer; Morgan Walters, media researcher;
Katy LaVigne, production specialist

Photo Credits
Corbis: Jeffrey Coolidge, (locker) bottom 49, Rick Friedman, 34, Roger Ressmeyer, 16;
Library of Congress: Gladstone Collection of African American Photographs, (vintage
photo) 37; Newscom: Melissa Lyttle/ZUMA Press, 55, NATIONAL WOMENS HALL
OF FAME, (alcott) top left 26, Richie Buxo, 59; Shutterstock: Claire McAdams, 30, Ivan
Kruk, 32, 0mela, 54, 33333, (marshmellows) top left 56, Africa Studio, (books) 26, alongzo,
38, amiloslava, (hand) 17, anawat sudchanham, 5, antoniodiaz, 23, Artex67, 43, Asier
Romero, (girl) 37, AtthameeNi, 48, blue67design, 61, Candus Camera, 60, CREATISTA,
21, 22, Curioso, 61, dimitris_k, 8, East, 10, EkaterinaP, background 13, Elise Gravel, Cover,
Elizaveta Ruzanova, 47, enciktat, (girls) top 33, evarin20, 50, hans.slegers, top 4, IrinaK,
14-15, isaxar, 53, Lena Pan, 40, Louella938, (crackers) middle right 56, Luis Molinero,
46, Maciej Sojka, 9, Macrovector, (books) 7, Maridav, 24, Marina Zezelina, (winter
scene) 44-45, maverick_infanta, (animals) 52, Michael Pettigrew, (child & dog) bottom
right 56, Nelosa, (hands) bottom 33, Nomad_Soul, (girl) top right 56, Ohmega1982,
(writing) background 17, Oleksandr Kostiuchenko, 12, Piotr Marcinski, 13, 19, Piti
Tan, 11, Raisman, 57, Rawpixel, 35, Ron Leishman, 42, savitskaya iryna, background 4,
25, sbego, 41, sumire8, (cards) 6, Sunny studio, (kid) bottom left 56, Tati Nova photo
Mexico, (woman) top 49, Tatiana Kholina, 29, View Apart, background 6-7; Wikimedia:
photographer's name, 39, Russell Watkins, 28

Printed in the United States of America in North Mankato, Minnesota.
062015   008823CGF15

TABLE OF CONTENTS

Introduction

"Believe me."

That message lives at the core of every piece of nonfiction. It doesn't matter whether you're writing about flip-flops, amoebas, your broken heart, or World War II. Nonfiction honors truth. It's based on observations, research, or memory. As a nonfiction writer, you believe what you're writing is true. You're asking your reader to believe you too.

More than any other genre, nonfiction comes in a dazzling array of forms. If you've ever read a newspaper article, a biography, or an encyclopedia article, you've read nonfiction. Essays on cooking, travel, or what someone thinks of their new laptop or notebook, are all nonfiction. So are letters, social media posts, and opinion pieces. And there's more!

Some nonfiction aims toward a specific purpose. It makes a case, explains an idea, or simply records what happened. Creative nonfiction reads like fiction but tells a true story. It's the best of both worlds!

Nonfiction writers look fearlessly at the way things are. They ask truth to lead them to prose that's useful, surprising, funny, compelling, and astonishing—sometimes all at once. Writing nonfiction is difficult and joyful work. Are you ready to get started?

"We write to discover what we think."

-Joan Didion, award-winning nonfiction writer

Chapter 1

Details, Details

Most of the time, we see the world as if we're looking out the windshield of a moving car. A drive to the store blurs by: tree, house, car, sidewalk, car, car, curb. But what if you stopped and really looked at one of those cars? You'd see bumper stickers, dents, and scratches. You'd see a puddle of coffee on the dashboard. It drips onto a stack of handwritten papers ... a letter? What kind of letter? One detail leads to another. Soon they start to tell a story.

Details are the building blocks of nonfiction. They make your writing vivid, believable, and interesting. A fiction writer invents details. Your job is to notice them and choose the best ones to tell your story.

"Instructions for living a life:
Pay attention.
Be astonished.
Tell about it."

-Mary Oliver, American poet and essayist

So Much to See

Train your eyes to see the amazing details inside ordinary things. Cut a square out of an index card to make a 1-inch (2.5 cm) window. Prop up your frame. Write as much as you can about exactly what's inside it. Don't try to make it good—just notice. Think of contrasts, colors, shapes, light, and textures. Practice putting different things inside your frame—your sister's eye, the tip of a dog's tail, the handle of a cup, or the side of a book.

THE SIDE OF MY BOOK

The side of my book is a stack of lines. Hair-thin parallel lines, one for each page. Some are darker than others. The lines are fuzzy and gray at one end. The book's glossy, yellow cover curls away from the pages, not quite touching. It casts a curved shadow over the pages below, dividing the stack into dark and light.

Interesting, Odd, Beautiful

Imagine walking down a rocky beach. Your eyes scan hundreds of gray pebbles and broken shells. You pass over these ordinary pieces in search of a real beauty—sea-polished glass or a multicolored rock.

When you are writing nonfiction, selecting details is a lot like picking up treasures on the beach. There are many possible details you could add to your writing to paint a picture in your readers' minds. On the beach, you stay open to any discovery but pocket only those prizes that are most interesting, odd, or beautiful.

Similarly, on the page, you want to include the very best details. Like beach treasures, they may take a little more time to collect, but the result is a rich, one-of-a-kind description that highlights your unique view on the world.

YOUR TURN

What interesting, odd, or beautiful details can you observe in this picture? Write a paragraph or two describing what you see, including five details that other people might not notice without your help.

Bonus challenge: Try this exercise again, but this time choose a picture you know well. You'll need to be extra observant to find new, interesting details in a photo you've seen many times.

The Telling Detail

So you're writing about your latest crush, Josh. You love how awkward he is. It's part of his charm! But how do you put his unique qualities into words?

Think of everything you could describe about Josh. You could mention his style-less style, his scuffed shoes, his free-falling hair, the angles of his face, his voice, and more. But wait—these details might seem fascinating to you, but won't they put readers to sleep? Do your readers a favor! Instead of cataloging every single detail you notice about Josh, choose just one or two choice descriptions, or telling details.

Telling details do double duty. They describe, but they also suggest. They point to a deeper meaning beyond what's at hand. Telling details are precise, vivid, and memorable.

So tell about the teeth marks in Josh's glasses. Tell about how he picks at his calloused palms while he talks. Why does he chew on his glasses? What made his hands calloused? A telling detail prompts the reader's curiosity and makes them want to know more.

"You do not have to explain every single drop of water contained in a rain barrel. You have to explain one drop—H_2O. The reader will get it."

-George Singleton, American author

Go to a public place and observe five people. Write down three interesting details about each one. Then write down what each detail might suggest about the person. Take a second look at the man in a shirt and tie with sweat dripping down his face. Was he just working out? Or maybe he has received terrible news. Notice the woman with earrings that are just slightly mismatched. Is she colorblind, absentminded, or just really busy? What about the teenage boy texting without looking down at his phone?

After you're done making observations, choose your most telling detail for each person. What made it stand out from the others?

Gather and Cut

First you gather up tons of observations, then you take most of them away. That's how nonfiction writers generate the best details. It's a lot of work. Good thing it's also tons of fun.

Think of a memorable meal you've had with someone. Next, expand the sentence, "We ate together" with as many details as you can. Really go for it, so your paragraph looks something like this:

On a misty July morning, while the rain evaporated, molecule by molecule, into a blue sky of daydreams, I followed you to a thorny patch of raspberries. "C'mon!" you yelled back to me. The humid air rubbed against our skin like a purring cat. Our feet sank and popped with each muddy step. Bending, we shook the soft, ripe, pink berries into our open mouths. "Mmmmmmmm," we chorused. "So good!" The berries practically sprang from their branches. We squatted in the dirt like toddlers. We crushed the raspberries with our tongues, letting the sweet juice spill down our throats like prehistoric animals. Some fell onto our faces, leaving pink stains on our cheeks. You looked like you'd been laughing raspberry tears. Completely satisfied, we traced our muddy footsteps back. Dirt stains crawled from our ankles to our elbows, while thin, red scratches played tic-tac-toe over our bare shins. Our cheeks stayed pink for days.

Now, go through your description and circle the best details. Cross out anything vague, repetitive, or unnecessary. Edit your paragraph down by half or more:

Under a blue sky of daydreams, I followed you to a raspberry patch. Our feet sank and popped with each muddy step. We squatted under thorny branches, shaking berries into our open mouths. We crushed them with our tongues like prehistoric animals. Dirt crawled from our ankles to our elbows, while scratches played tic-tac-toe on our shins. Our cheeks stayed pink for days.

Do you see how this edit focuses on imagery of kids playing? Without extra details, the messy fun of the meal shines through.

Writing about your experiences is nothing new. People have been doing it for hundreds of years. Take Catherine Haun, for example. She kept her eye for sharp detail as she traveled in a wagon across the Great Plains in 1849. Haun kept her eye for detail sharp as she traveled in a wagon across the Great Plains. In 1849, Haun described running into a buffalo herd in her journal.

Getting to Know: Catherine Haun

"A Herd of Buffalo"

Finally after a couple of weeks' travel the distant mountains of the west came into view.

This was the land of the buffalo. One day a herd came in our direction like a great black cloud, a threatening moving mountain, advancing towards us very swiftly and with wild snorts, noses almost to the ground and tails flying in midair. I haven't any idea how many there were but they seemed to be innumerable and made a deafening terrible noise. As is their habit, when stampeding, they did not turn out of their course for anything. Some of our wagons were within their line of advance and in consequence one was completely demolished and two were overturned. Several persons were hurt, one child's shoulder being dislocated, but fortunately no one was killed.

Two of these buffaloes were shot and the humps and tongues furnished us with fine fresh meat. They happened to be buffalo cows and, in consequence, the meat was particularly good flavor and tender. It is believed that the cow can run faster than the bull. The large bone of the hind leg, after being stripped of the flesh, was buried in coals of buffalo chips and in an hour the baked marrow was served. I have never tasted such a rich, delicious food!

Look for fascinating images of frontier life on the Internet or at your local museum. Write a description of one of the scenes as if you were a young pioneer like Catherine Haun.

AUTHOR PROFILE:

Paul Zindel

YA author Paul Zindel wrote an acclaimed memoir about his troubled years growing up in Staten Island, New York, in the 1940s. *The Pigman & Me* focuses on a friendship between young Paul and a grandfatherly Italian man, Nonno Frankie, who showed a remarkable zest for life.

Paul met Nonno Frankie in the shared backyard of his family house. Through telling detail, Paul vividly shows the old man's playful spirit:

"He stood up, sniffed at the earth in his hands, then breathed in deeply like he was sampling a French perfume. He began checking out every square inch of the backyard. His billowing plaid shirt flickered against his belly, and he wore brown baggy pants like a clown's."

Chapter 2

Storyteller's Tricks

Nonfiction storytellers try to make their stories as vivid in their readers' minds as in their own minds. Some people are natural storytellers. They have the audience on a thread without even knowing what they are doing. If it doesn't come naturally, no need to stress. Some tried and true tricks can help bring out the captivating storyteller in everyone.

Visualize!

Imagine your friend Madison is telling you a true story from her life. She sends you this text:

Got high score in history.
Mr. Swan so embarrassing about it!

Ho-hum. You had to be there, right?

But what if Madison rewrote her text as a scene that brought the event to life?

"Ladies and gentlemen, may I have your attention?" Mr. Swan boomed out during sixth-period history. "I have an announcement regarding your fellow scholar, Madison Monroe!" He peered down at me over the top of his little round glasses. He was holding a rolled-up paper in his hand. He waved it over my head like my fairy godfather.

"Drumroll, ple-eeee-ase!" he sang out.

My classmates attacked their desks with pencils, while I slumped deeper in my seat.

Mr. Swan's eyes twinkled at me, and I thought to myself how much he looked like Santa. With a flick of his wrist, he unfurled his mysterious scroll.

"Ninety-nine!" Mr. Swan read aloud the neon pink numbers on the top of the page. "The highest grade on last week's test!" His cheeks turned merry and bright. "Congratulations!" he grabbed my hand and shook my arm. "Ms. Monroe, would you like to share a few words with your classmates?"

"Um, thank you? Really, thanks so much," I murmured, hoping to turn invisible. "I'm speechless."

Madison's new story is an example of narrative nonfiction. She's using storytelling tricks such as dialogue to show the quirkiness of Mr. Swan's personality. His actions—the way he waves the scroll like a fairy godfather—add to his characterization. She gives a sense of her own point of view—what she was thinking and feeling during the event. Madison's text reported the event, but her scene shows what happened, as if we are seeing it in a movie.

"Let the world burn through you. Throw the prism light, white hot, on paper."

—Ray Bradbury, author of *The Martian Chronicles*

YOUR TURN

FROM SENTENCE TO SCENE

Now you try to craft a scene between you and one other main character. Think of a time someone embarrassed you, or made you angry, sad, or happy. Write down what happened in one or two sentences:

Miranda said she's not my friend anymore.
Henry invited me to sit with him at lunch.
My mom hugged me in front of my friends.

Next close your eyes and try to remember everything you can about the event. What did the two of you say? Where were you? What were the other person's expressions and gestures? What were you thinking and feeling during the conversation?

Turn your sentence into a scene with dialogue, action, and your point of view. Make it so vivid that you'll be able to live the event all over again.

Bonus challenge: Write the scene again, but flip the point of view. The other character is now the "I." See the story through their eyes instead of yours. Stretch your imagination and put yourself in their shoes.

Eavesdropping for Dialogue

Are you nosy? Do you have an "ear" for details? Good! That will help you write better nonfiction dialogue. The best written speech sounds natural, which can be hard to pull off. You have to train your ears by listening—really listening—to how people talk.

Good nonfiction writers notice what people say and how they say it. Do most people speak in complete sentences or fragments? Do they interrupt? How do people talk differently to children, to their friends, to strangers? What makes someone sound odd, excited, sad, or thoughtful?

Make a habit of eavesdropping on people in public places. Write down what you hear. (If your head is in a notebook, no one will suspect you're listening in!) Notice their gestures, expressions, and habits. Don't worry about getting everything down exactly. You can fill in the details later.

Once you've collected a dozen or so conversations, pick your favorite. Turn it into a scene by choosing just the most interesting bits of dialogue. Break up the speech with actions and telling details to make your scene even more vivid.

Bring Them to Life

What is your best friend like? Is she kind, thoughtful, fun, smart, or a little bit goofy? Those adjectives may mean a lot to you, but they don't add up to much for someone who has never met her.

We need examples.

Thoughtful how?

"She's always the first one to call me on my birthday."

Goofy how?

"She forgets to set her alarm in the morning."

Developing characters in nonfiction is a lot like talking about a good friend. First you need to understand your character. You know their talents and flaws, worries and triumphs. You get what drives them. Second, you show your unique insight through examples that bring them to life.

Think about someone you know very well, like a close friend or sibling. Complete this sentence:

_ _ _ _ _ _ _ _ is the most _ _ _ _ _ _ _ _ _ _ _ _ person I know.

Next, list five specific things they've said or done that show this trait. Choose the best one or two, and write a quick character sketch. Here's an example:

My sister is the most outgoing person I know. When she was two, she'd press her face against the screen door and shout "Hi!" at every stranger. If they didn't wave back, she'd break down in tears.

Bonus challenge: Ask the person you chose to write a character sketch about you too. Then read each other's papers. What do they think of what you wrote? Did their sketch capture something about you?

Chapter 3

True Confessions

Writing Memoir

Memoir comes from the French word for memory, *mémoire*. A memoir is a true story, told in the first person "I," based on the writer's own memory. Memoir writers care about the facts and believe deeply in the truth of what they are writing. Often they base their work on diaries, or they do extensive research to back up their memories.

Unlike an autobiography, a memoir does not document a person's entire life. It focuses on just a slice—a specific challenge or times of change. How the author remembers his or her past is just as important as what happened. Memoir writers look in the shadows and corners of their lives to reveal truths that are both surprising and familiar. The process can be awkward, uncomfortable, or downright frightening.

Another challenge is that memories aren't always 100 percent accurate. Sometimes there's no way to verify the facts. For example, a memoir writer may describe her ruined party dress as black satin because that's how she remembered it. Perhaps the dress was actually deep purple, but if there's no way to know for sure, the best the writer can do is be true to her memory.

> "I write as a witness to what I have seen. I write as a witness to what I imagine."
>
> -Terry Tempest Williams, American author

AUTHOR PROFILE:

Louisa May Alcott

Louisa May Alcott (1832–1888) is most famous for writing the classic novel *Little Women*, but she was an avid nonfiction writer too. Even as a girl, she wrote hundreds of letters and diary entries. When she was 17, she poured her heart out about how it felt to be compared to her older sister, Anna.

Getting to Know: Louisa May Alcott

"Louisa's Diary"

BOSTON, May, 1850.–So long a time has passed since I kept a journal that I hardly know how to begin. ... Seventeen years have I lived, and yet so little do I know, and so much remains to be done before I begin to be what I desire–a truly good and useful woman.

In looking over our journals, Father says, "Anna's is about other people, Louisa's about herself." That is true, for I don't talk about myself; yet must always think of the willful, moody girl I try to manage, and in my journal I write of her to see how she gets on. Anna is so good she need not take care of herself, and can enjoy other people. If I look in my glass, I try to keep down vanity about my long hair, my well-shaped head, and my good nose. In the street I try not to covet fine things. My quick tongue is always getting me into trouble, and my moodiness makes it hard to be cheerful when I think how poor we are, how much worry it is to live, and how many things I long to do I never can.

YOUR TURN

Do you have aspects of your personality that you keep hidden? Do you have a secret person inside that you have to "manage"? How is that person different from the image you project in the world? Write an entry in your diary about the true you.

AUTHOR PROFILE:

Malala Yousafzai

On October 9, 2012, Malala Yousafzai was riding home from her school in northwest Pakistan when two armed men stormed the bus. "Who is Malala?" they asked. Though just a teenager, Malala was well known in Pakistan and, increasingly, around the world. She was an outspoken advocate for girls' education, a right that was threatened by Taliban terrorists. As a result of her activism, a Taliban gunman shot her in the head. After many months, Malala recovered and continued her work as an activist. In 2014, at age 17, she became the youngest person ever to receive a Nobel Peace Prize. She also published the YA version of her bestselling memoir, *I Am Malala: How One Girl Stood Up for Education and Changed the World*.

"Yes, the Taliban have shot me," Malala wrote. "But they can only shoot a body. They cannot shoot my dreams."

Malala ends her inspiring story with her dreams for the future: "Peace in every home, every street, every village, every country—that is my dream. Education for every boy and every girl in the world. To sit down on a chair and read my books with all my friends at school is my right. To see each and every human being with a smile of true happiness is my wish."

YOUR TURN

What is your dream? Write a paragraph about a dream you would be willing to put yourself in danger to achieve.

I Like to Move It, Move It!

A bowl of chocolates reminds you of getting sick on Halloween, right on your tap shoes. That makes you think of last year's recital, and that in turn reminds you of that song you danced to, about the moon ...

Let's face it—our memories don't always occur in order, and neither do memoirs, necessarily. They can be strange and wandering, just like memory itself.

It's OK to let memories flow organically. Arranging events in the order they happened is a predictable story plot. Why not try mixing up things a little to keep your reader guessing?

Putting two non-chronological events side-by-side can highlight differences between them. On the other hand, it can also draw out the similarities between two scenes. The organization of your nonfiction can also help readers draw conclusions they may not have thought of otherwise.

So how do you do it? Well, you might write one chunk of memoir at a time, piece by piece, in the order in which they occur to you. Once the whole story is written, take a second look and rearrange as needed. Or you might write everything chronologically, then rearrange things afterward. Whatever works best for you is the best practice to follow.

Write your own experimental memoir on four index cards, writing just a few sentences on each card.

Card 1: Think of a smell from your past. Is it sour, sweet, sharp, or fresh? It might be from a day outside, a favorite food, or a time when you were sick. Describe the smell and what it reminds you of.

Card 2: Describe the eyes of someone you love: "My grandma's eyes are gray and watery. Wrinkles fan out from the corners. They squint into slits when she laughs."

Card 3: Write a remark that you hear all the time, either at school or in your family. It can be anything. "No dessert until you've eaten your veggies." "Goodnight, my angel." Or, "Be a good example for your brother."

Card 4: Think back on an important first in your life. It might be your first day of school, the first time you flew on an airplane, or the first time you met your best friend. Quickly list 10 nouns (specific physical things or people) about that memory. Your first time at the beach might begin like this: sunscreen, sandy footprints, Mom's sunglasses, tears, Port-A-Potty, salty waves ...

Shuffle your cards, and write a title for each one. Read your memoir out loud, including the titles. You've created a nonfiction word collage. What interesting connections and comparisons do you notice?

Secrets and Consideration

Memoirs are our stories about our lives, told just as we remember them. A host of other characters—family members, friends, teachers, neighbors, and more—appear in memoirs. Why is this important, you ask? If you portray a someone in a negative way in your memoir, he or she may feel upset if you share the story with others. Also, some people are very private. Revealing details of their lives may make them uncomfortable.

It's smart to think about who will be reading or hearing your work. If you write that your brother can't add up to five, and he's older than five—he may be very upset. If you write about a teacher you had a crush on in third grade and it's published in the school literary journal, that might embarrass you. Or him.

A good rule of thumb is not to publish or share writing that makes anyone look bad. Does that mean you should stop writing blazingly honest material? Not at all. You have every right to express yourself in your writing. The key is to be sure you distinguish between the writing you will share with others and the writing that is done for your personal experience and benefit—in your diary. Tell your story, but be considerate, honest, and fair.

AUTHOR PROFILE:

Jack Gantos

> "I have learned this: it is not what one does that is wrong, but what one becomes as a consequence of it."
>
> Oscar Wilde, 19th century playwright

Jack Gantos chose this famous quote by Oscar Wilde to set the stage for his memoir, *Hole in My Life.* The best-selling young adult author recounts how, as a desperate teenager, he took a job smuggling drugs that landed him in prison. His life as a writer began there as he scribbled a secret diary between the lines of a prison library book.

In high school Jack had searched endlessly for "juicy" subjects to fill his journal. But he lacked the confidence and patience to see the opportunities right in front of him. "In prison I got a second chance to realize I did have something to write about."

> "If I don't write to empty my mind, I go mad."
>
> -19th-century poet Lord Byron

Chapter 4

Prose with a Purpose

Want to sell something online? Invite a friend to a party? Explain how to craft a Duct Tape wallet, review a book you love, or convince your classmates to elect your best friend for student council? Count on nonfiction when you have a job to do, such as guide, explain, advise, or make a point.

"Don't try to figure out what other people want to hear from you; figure out what you have to say. It's the one and only thing you have to offer."

-Barbara Kingsolver, American novelist, essayist, and poet

Getting to Know: Sojourner Truth

"Ain't I a woman?"

You may have heard of Sojourner Truth in history class. A former slave, Sojourner was an important voice in the abolitionist movement and a fierce advocate for women's rights. Sojourner never learned to read or write, but she showed a remarkable flair for words. In 1851, she delivered a speech at the Women's Convention in Akron, Ohio, that she made up on the spot. As men in the audience heckled and jeered, Sojourner made the point that women were equal to men, using her own experiences as a slave to prove her point.

That man over there says that women need to be helped into carriages, and lifted over ditches, and to have the best place everywhere. Nobody ever helps me into carriages, or over mud-puddles, or gives me any best place! And ain't I a woman? Look at me! Look at my arm! I have ploughed and planted, and gathered into barns, and no man could head me! And ain't I a woman? I could work as much and eat as much as a man—when I could get it—and bear the lash as well! And ain't I a woman? I have borne thirteen children, and seen most all sold off to slavery, and when I cried out with my mother's grief, none but Jesus heard me! And ain't I a woman?

I Sell the Shadow to Support the Substance.
SOJOURNER TRUTH.

YOUR TURN

"Ain't I a woman?" is an example of a rhetorical question. Sojourner wasn't expecting an answer—she repeated the question to make a point. Write your own speech that makes a point by using a repeating rhetorical question.

First, choose an issue you care about. It could be a social issue such as the environment, women's rights, or homelessness. Or write about something that affects you personally, such as a school policy or a family rule.

Second, find a rhetorical question. Choose from this list, or make up your own:

Why not?
Who says so?
Why can't we change?
How much longer?
Since when?

David Macaulay

David Macaulay is a children's book author and illustrator who follows his curiosity wherever it takes him. He creates lavishly illustrated books that explain how things work, from an old cathedral to modern technology. His three goals for every book are that they be clear, accurate, and engaging.

Macaulay knows very little about a subject when he begins. *The Way We Work*, about the human body, was no exception. Macaulay spent six years on the book, filling up 10 books of notes along the way. He took anatomy courses and observed live surgeries. He felt and sketched real organs in a lab.

Pick an organ that you know practically nothing about—maybe your spleen, gall bladder, or pancreas. Find out how it works. Write a paragraph explaining how it works. Draw pictures with labels and arrows, just for fun.

Sell It

Writers have a way with words. Nonfiction writers can use their skills in very practical ways. For example, if you were to write an online ad selling something you own, your writing skills would help you to get a great response.

When writing persuasive text, whether it's an essay or an ad, first ask yourself what would be the strongest, most enticing ways to make your point. Brainstorm at least five strong points, then pick your favorite and make that the focus of your headline. After you grab the reader's attention with a killer headline, follow it up with specific details in the body of the ad. When you can flex your writing skills in a practical way, you'll have buyers begging for your hand-me-downs!

CUTE-AS-A-BUNNY WINTER HAT

White knit hat with bunny ears, purchased last fall from a street vendor in Uptown. So soft you'll want to hug it. Silky pink lining keeps it 100 percent itch-free. Ears tie under the chin for extra-chilly emergencies. Kept me warm when bus was 30 minutes late last January! $45, or highest bidder. Cash only, please.

Think of your teacher's rules at school. Perhaps they include such things as:

Pay attention.

Be organized.

Do your homework.

Those rules are tried-and-true for succeeding in school. But what about the other rules? The little-known rules that only the kids at your school know?

Don't eat the cottage cheese in the salad bar.

You can take your shoes off in Ms. Walker's class.

Avoid the second-floor water fountain—it sprays your feet.

Imagine that you are helping a new transfer student at your school get adjusted. What 10 things will he or she need to know to feel like part of the group? Write a guide to your school's special rules.

Be Convincing

Are you persuaded that these meals were awful by this description?

"The daily lunches at my elementary school's cafeteria were easily the most vile meals I've ever experienced. My unlucky classmates and I were often the recipients of overcooked goulash, an acidic tomato-and-pasta disaster baked into a putty-like form. Gravy on bread was another doozy. The slimy, yellowish-gray gravy was ladled onto a piece of white bread. Even the macaroni and cheese was off-colored. It tasted like the first ingredient might just be glue. Even the smell of the cafeteria was enough to unsettle my otherwise rumbling tummy."

Are there meals you dread? Movies you'd just as soon skip to do homework? Or what about things you love?

YOUR TURN

Writing a review can be a great way to practice writing creative descriptions. Write a review of your own. When you've finished, go back and circle your favorite descriptions and phrases. Why are they your favorites? Keep the review as possible material for later work.

Chapter 5

Voice Experiments

Compare these three descriptions:

All day long, snowflakes fell from the gray sky.

The snow fell and it fell and it fell. Icy flakes from a dishwater sky.

The snowflakes swirled and swooped like dancers. Their stage was the winter sky.

These three descriptions basically say the same thing, right? It snowed a lot. But each one feels so different. Each has its own voice that conveys a distinct tone.

In these examples, notice how much the mood shifted by changing word choice, sentence structure, and images. "Winter sky" sounds lovely, while "dishwater sky" feels depressing. Rhythms and sounds affect voice, too. "Snowflakes swirl and swoop" sounds playful and light. "The snow fell and it fell and it fell" sounds dreary and monotonous.

You can make your voice stark, serious, strange, sarcastic, angry, aloof, funny, over-the-top, and so much more. In nonfiction, the reader understands that the voice comes from you, the author, not any other character. Your voice is a window into your true thoughts and feelings.

1, 2, 3, Change It!

How do you develop your voice as a writer? Read like crazy. Read your favorite passages aloud. Look closely at the word choice and sentence structures. Let the music of the language train your ear. Read aloud if that helps.

Experiment, experiment, experiment! Don't ever be afraid to change your words. Just hold on to your drafts, so you can always change your words back.

Choose a paragraph from your diary, a school essay, an e-mail, or any piece of nonfiction you have written. Rewrite it to change the voice. Remember—change only words, rhythms, and images. The content stays the same. Pick three voices from this list and go:

- childish
- stuffy
- depressing
- annoying
- excited
- creepy
- devastated
- half-asleep
- emotional

You're not done yet. Rewrite your original paragraph three times. Don't worry about whether it's good—just change as much as you can. In the first draft, change your sentence structures. Break up sentences and combine them. Move words and clauses around. "He danced and laughed" becomes "He laughed and danced."

In your second draft, swap out as many words as you can. "He danced and laughed" becomes "He twirled and giggled."

Third, add in as many images as you can squeeze in there. "He danced like a kid on a pogo stick." "His head flew back as he laughed."

Review your results. How did your changes affect the tone of the paragraph? What changes would you keep, and what would you change back?

Break the Rules

Your teachers have instructed you in the rules of writing: Don't use sentence fragments. Avoid run-on sentences. Vary your sentence structures. Those trusty rules will steer your right for most of your writing. But sometimes, creative writers break rules for special occasions.

In the essay "Pop Art," Brian Doyle, an award-winning Canadian children's author, describes what he's learned about his three children:

They are engines of incalculable joy and agonizing despair. They are comedy machines. Their language is their own and the order of their new halting words has never been heard before in the whole history of the world. They are headlong and hilarious. Their hearts are enormous and sensitive beyond human calculation.

YOUR TURN

Think of somebody who intrigues you. It could be a teacher, coach, relative, famous person, or friend. Make a list of everything you've learned about him or her. Write your notes into a paragraph with sentences that all start with she/her or he/him.

Bonus Challenge: Use sentence fragments to write about a dream you can only half-remember or a time when your thoughts were racing. Use run-on sentences to write about something that's really messy, like your room or a friend's locker.

Hook 'Em!

Which of these essays about cats would you rather read—sample A or sample B?

A. Cats are such amazing animals. They're so different from dogs. They're different from what you'd expect. You'll be really surprised when you read about these cat facts …

B. True or false?
A cat can jump up to six times the length of its body.
A cat can make 100 different sounds, while dogs make only 10.
Cats sweat through their feet.
The answers are true, true, and true. Read on, and learn what makes cats so amazing.

OK, that was easy. You picked Sample B, right? The author of that essay used a hook in her introduction to grab your interest and make you want to read more. In this case, she used startling information to hook you. That's just one successful strategy. Here are some others ways to hook a reader:

START WITH A STORY

My cat Doodle once got me kicked out of school. True story. He climbed into my backpack and fell asleep. When I unzipped my bag in homeroom, out jumped a spitting, hissing, furry monster. Doodle sprang off my desk and jumped, at least six times the length of his body. He landed right in Ms. Laugerman's lap.

START WITH A QUOTE

"Not all those who wander are lost." When J.R.R. Tolkien wrote that famous line, I think he had a cat in mind. Cats are survival machines who claim their homes wherever they feel like it.

ASK QUESTIONS

What would you do if you could jump six times the length of your body? What if you could see seven times better in the dark? What if you ears could rotate 180 degrees? You'd be a cat.

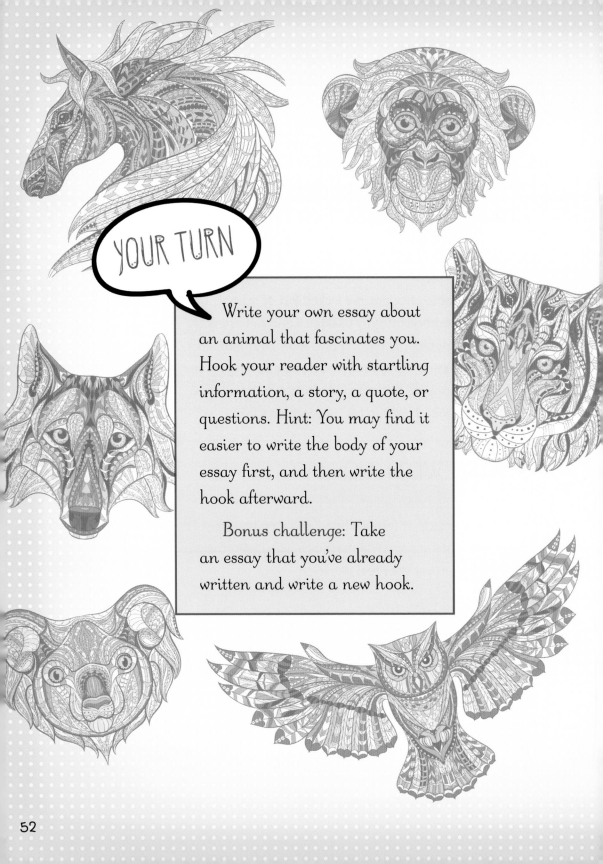

YOUR TURN

Write your own essay about an animal that fascinates you. Hook your reader with startling information, a story, a quote, or questions. Hint: You may find it easier to write the body of your essay first, and then write the hook afterward.

Bonus challenge: Take an essay that you've already written and write a new hook.

Chapter 6

Jump Starts!

It's happened to every writer. You have an idea about something you want to write about. But when you sit down to do it, words don't come. Or if they do come, you delete them right away. Either way, you're facing a blank screen.

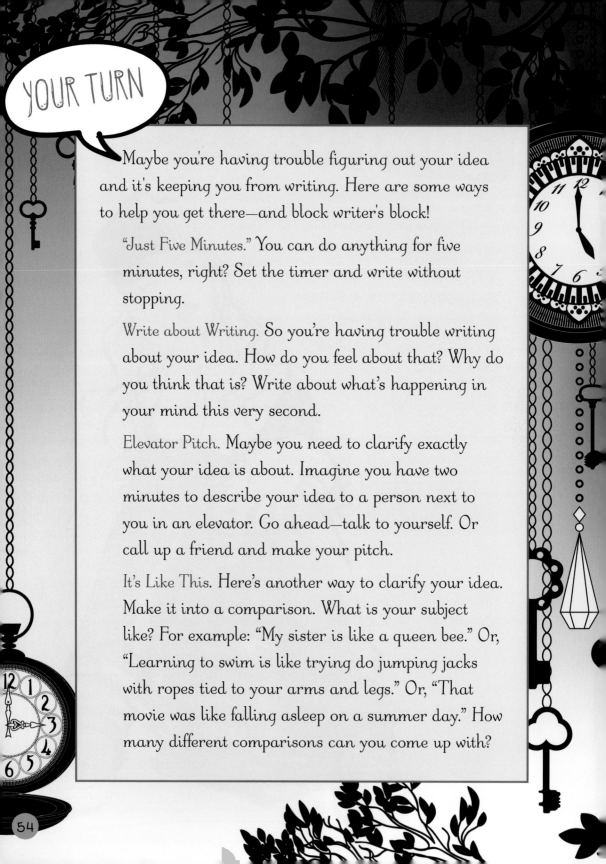

YOUR TURN

Maybe you're having trouble figuring out your idea and it's keeping you from writing. Here are some ways to help you get there—and block writer's block!

"Just Five Minutes." You can do anything for five minutes, right? Set the timer and write without stopping.

Write about Writing. So you're having trouble writing about your idea. How do you feel about that? Why do you think that is? Write about what's happening in your mind this very second.

Elevator Pitch. Maybe you need to clarify exactly what your idea is about. Imagine you have two minutes to describe your idea to a person next to you in an elevator. Go ahead—talk to yourself. Or call up a friend and make your pitch.

It's Like This. Here's another way to clarify your idea. Make it into a comparison. What is your subject like? For example: "My sister is like a queen bee." Or, "Learning to swim is like trying do jumping jacks with ropes tied to your arms and legs." Or, "That movie was like falling asleep on a summer day." How many different comparisons can you come up with?

AUTHOR PROFILE:

Ashley Rhodes-Courter

"I have had more than a dozen so-called mothers in my life," Ashley Rhodes-Courter begins her memoir, *Three Little Words*. Ashley was just 22 years old when her true story of life in Florida's foster care system hit the *New York Times* bestseller list. From ages 3 to 12, Ashley was shuttled between 9 schools and 14 foster families. At one point, she lived in a two-bedroom trailer with 16 other children. Almost one-quarter of her foster parents were or became convicted felons.

Ashley recounts vivid scenes from her very early childhood. To do so, she conducted extensive research. She reviewed her government records and sifted through photos. She traveled back to her former foster homes and interviewed past contacts.

Think back to one of your earliest memories. Write about it in a scene with dialogue and action. Interview family members and look through old photos to bring it to life.

List Away

One of the best ways to get your pen scratching is simply to make a list. List three fun things you did today. List your favorite movies, books, and games. What are the five foods that make you gag? Six things you secretly like but would never admit? Eight songs you wish you could erase from your head?

Five Funny Things I Believed When I Was Little:

1. The moon followed me wherever I went.

2. Squirrels would crawl on me if I pretended I was a tree.

3. A graham cracker made a good bookmark.

4. My dog was related to me.

5. Marshmallows were berries that grew on marshmallow bushes.

Make a list of things you'd like to write about. When you are stumped about what to write, revisit your list to get the creative juices flowing. Simpy pick your favorite, and write away!

Bonus challenge: Illustrate your list with old photos, clip art, or free images from the web.

"If it sounds like writing, I rewrite it. Or, if proper usage gets in the way, it may have to go. I can't allow what we learned in English composition to disrupt the sound and rhythm of the narrative."

-Elmore Leonard, American novelist and screenwriter

"If they give you ruled paper, write the other way."

-Juan Ramón Jiménez, Nobel-prize winning Spanish poet

The Short Memoir and Flash Nonfiction

Six-Word Memoir

"If you had exactly six words to describe your life, what would they be?"

For more than six years, the editors of the Six-Word Memoir Project have been asking people that question. In several print and online collections, people from all around the world have written and shared their entire lives in six words. Whether silly, sad, or poignant, a six-word memoir can be a challenge to write.

HERE ARE SOME REAL SIX-WORD MEMOIRS FROM KIDS
IN MIDDLE SCHOOL:

Fit in or be tossed out.

Not as strong as I pretend.

Drawing is my airplane to imagination.

Quiet, shy, give me a try.

I can't survive without ice cream.

AUTHOR PROFILE:

Tavi Gevinson

At age 11, Tavi Gevinson was looking for an outlet for all her creative ideas and opinions. With a "why not?" attitude she started her own fashion blog, Style Rookie. She posted pictures of her outfits and commented on the latest fashion trends. Months later, Tavi's blog had gone viral. She found herself on all-expense-paid trips to fashion shows in New York and Paris.

In 2011, at age 15, Tavi started her own online magazine for teen girls. These days, *Rookie* gets some 3.5 million hits a month. Funky and feminist, the lifestyle magazine features everything from personal essays and music reviews to DIY craft guides and celebrity interviews. The best part? A lot of the articles come from readers.

Writing Flash Nonfiction

It's like nonfiction, but bite size! Writing flash nonfiction is often tricky, especially for people who love to write. Even though you are usually advised to write more, for this exercise, limit your entire nonfiction story to 10 to 12 sentences.

The challenge of presenting a poignant event in so few sentences can push your writing and revision skills to a new level. Flash writing forces you to use crisp, precise language with no thoughtless repetition. When you have a strict limit, each word becomes more important. Choosing the best, freshest words possible is half the battle. Choosing a good topic is the other, so brainstorm a list of ideas first. Then, choose your favorite topic and give it a try.

Flash Nonfiction: Take a Look

In case you can't think of one, here's an example to use as a springboard:

What was it like? That's what everyone keeps asking me. Imagine climbing to the highest building in the world. No elevator; you took the stairs for months. Finally, you climb onto the roof, where a roller coaster awaits you. You buckle in. Next thing you know, you're going 1,000 miles per hour in a loop that twists through nothing but sky and fireworks. You want to scream, laugh, cry, and throw up all at once. What was it like? It was like that, only more.

Works Cited

Louisa May Alcott, *Diary*
https://www.gutenberg.org/files/38049/38049-h/38049-h.htm#Page_56

Ambrose Bierce, *Devil's Dictionary*
https://www.gutenberg.org/files/972/972-h/972-h.htm

Catherine Haun, *"A Herd of Buffalo"*
http://www.wwnorton.com/college/history/eamerica/media/ch14/resources/documents/haun.htm

Six-Word Memoir Project
All entries from: http://www.sixwordmemoirs.com/schools/index.php

Sojourner Truth, *Ain't I a Woman?*
http://www.nps.gov/wori/learn/historyculture/sojourner-truth.htm

Glossary

autobiography (aw-toh-bye-OG-ruh-fee)—the true story of a writer's own life

blog (BLOG)—an online journal

character sketch (KAYR-ik-tur SKECH)—a short description of a character; it may include what they look like, how they act, and what drives them.

characterization (KA-rik-tuh-rize-ay-shun)—the process by which a writer tells about a character, including, for example, a character's speech and actions

collage (kuh-LAHZH)—art that is made by putting pieces of various materials together

dialogue (DYE-uh-log)—characters' conversations in a written work

draft (DRAFT)—a version of a piece of writing that is not yet finished

genre (ZHAHN-ruh)—a major category of writing

image (IM-ij)—descriptive language that sparks a vivid picture in the reader's mind

memoir (MEM-wohr)—a nonfiction story based on the writer's memories of his or her own life

metaphor (MET-uh-for)—a literary comparison between two things that, on the surface, may not seem alike at all

narrative nonfiction (NA-ruh-tiv NON-fik-shuhn)—a true story written in scenes with dialogue, action, and other literary techniques

objective (uhb-JEK-tiv)—not influenced by personal feelings; from a neutral point of view

outline (OUT-line)—a plan for a piece of writing

point of view (POINT UV VYOO)—the "eyes" through which the reader experiences what happens in a story; in a first person point of view, the reader experiences events through the author's own eyes.

prose (PROZE)—everyday writing

scene (SEEN)—a unit in a story that shows what happens in a distinct time and place; a scene is the opposite of a summary

telling detail (TELL-ing DEE-tale)—detail that not only describes a thing but also suggests something deeper about it

vivid (VIV-id)—producing precise, clear images in the mind

voice (VOISS)—an author's distinct writing style crafted through word choice, rhythms, sentence construction, and images.

Read More

Benke, Karen. *Rip the Page!: Adventures in Creative Writing*. Boston: Trumpeter, 2010.

Llanas, Sheila Griffin. *Picture Yourself Writing Fiction: Using Photos to Inspire Writing*. North Mankato, Minn.: Capstone Press, 2012.

Mazer, Anne, and **Ellen Potter**. *Spilling Ink: A Young Writer's Handbook*. New York: RB Flash Point/Roaring Brook Press, 2010.

Internet Sites

Use FactHound to find Internet sites related to this book.
All of the sites on FactHound have been researched by our staff.

Here's all you do:

Visit *www.facthound.com*

Type in this code: **9781491459898**

Index

About the Author

Nadia Higgins is the author of more than 80 nonfiction books for children and young adults, and she has personally used several of the tips and tricks in this book many times over. One of her favorite parts of being a nonfiction writer is figuring out how to organize all her facts in surprising or interesting ways. A die-hard researcher, Ms. Higgins has written about everything from ants to popsicles to zombies. She lives in Minneapolis, Minnesota, with her family.